Table of Contents

INTRODUCTION

I0408197

1.   Chapter One
       What the Hell Happened

2.   Chapter Two
       The Republican War Room

3.   Chapter Three
       Whack-a-dos Everywhere

4.   Chapter Four
       The Third-Party Messiness

5.   Chapter Five
       The Media and Bias

6.   Chapter Six
       What Democrats Must Change

7.   Chapter Seven
       Enough Racism, Prejudice, Bias to Go Around

8.   Chapter Eight
       The Russian Effect on 2016 Election

       Summary of 2016 Election

       *****
       Church
       Hollywood
       Past & Present Dangers

Dedication

To those who voted and are now regretting their 2016 vote.

This commentary is the expressed opinion of one person and references made are from news, reports, and articles already in print, some have been cited.

Volume I

To Hell in a Handbasket

Americas 2016 Election Catastrophe

by

Tracy T.B.

Introduction

No one said politics are clean and honest, and all elected officials care about their constituents—especially in America. Ladies and gentlemen, it's one of the biggest lies ever told. Now that we have a madman in office, which is fond of white nationalist, David Duke, KKK, Breitbart News, and Vladimir Putin, let me say it plainly: "America, we have a problem." In this book, you may see me use the word "we", but that in no way means that I voted, encouraged, or rallied behind the current President. I want to make that clear to the reader. Who I voted for is private.

We have never been infiltrated by a Russian oligarch like the one we currently have in the White House 2016. In my opinion, this is a new low. We have an elected President that won't say anything negative about a dictator that deserves it, one who has been deemed a ruthless communist leader.

And say No. 45 didn't have an idea that he was being used by Vladimir Putin's hate for Hillary Rodham Clinton, he still participated in the Putin scheme. He's pushed his hate into our American politics in a sneaky and underhanded way. Just like the way he has done in other countries. We have never seen a time when our military brass is taking orders based on what Vladimir Putin is telling the current Commander-In-Chief, No. 45, to do behind the scenes.

We have never seen a time when our Intel is being sucked right out of the White House by Russian spies. Then it's being disseminated by Julian Assange from WikiLeaks, who is a known rapist. What credibility does this man have over our country? We have never seen a time when a candidate for the President of the United States has more positive things to say about a Russian communist leader than he does about the democracy of our government here in the United States, which he now works under.

To make some sense of it all, I checked out 22 books at my local library so I could write in a coherent way about what I see as the worst entanglement that America (USA) has ever encountered. I have followed politics for over 50-years and never have I seen an overt coup da tat' like the deliberate and coordinated attack that we saw in the 2016 US election. It was like the media was being hit from all sides. They could not react or have the origins of the stories checked, and with the ones they did have, they did an ineffective job of investigative reporting.

I listened to the news cable every day, and I never heard one of them disparage or give any background about who Julian Assange is. He has been accused of drugging women and raping them. It was reported he raped three women in Sweden using drugs before he was banished and told to never come back. Then he ended up in Ecuador, stealing notes and spinning his evil Russian wheel there, working and getting paid by the Kremlin. The Guardian reported this about

Assange in December 2010 https://www.theguardian.com/media/2010/dec/17/julian-assange-sweden, and they point out the charges that were brought about for rape and why Assange has no credibility in regards to emails or WikiLeaks. Read it for yourself and determine on your own if you think Julian is trustworthy.

We must admit our flaws within our political system in the United States, which has been ravished with deceit at times. Richard Nixon manipulated the wars and the timeliness of certain actions during the Vietnam War. Secretary of State Henry Kissinger fixed it so that prisoners were being released only to hold them a little while longer until after the election. Our government does stuff like that when they want our votes. American voters don't realize that their votes are worth more than gold to a politician. All they want to do is get in office and get their government checks and great healthcare benefits. He can help his family, his friends, and keep his foes happy as well. It doesn't get any better than that.

It was the same scheme when Ronald Reagan ran against Jimmy Carter in (1972) and they manipulated the exit from the Vietnam War. Voters get very little out of these deals. And now that we have No. 45 as our President, we're going to hell in a handbasket quick. If the Democrats are not working as tirelessly as I am writing this short book to reconcile what happened to them in 2016, by the time four years is over, our country will no longer be remembered as the strongest country in the world. -

We are already a laughing stalk and being criticized for the "strangeness" of the person that 62 million Americans voted for. Even though No. 45 did not win the popular vote by 3,000,000 votes, the Republicans still won per the Electoral College votes. In other words, we were duped again like we were in 2002 when Al Gore lost to Republican George W. Bush, even after Dems got the popular vote. How long are we going to allow this trickery to continue? Enough should be enough!

This was a dog-eat-dog campaign by any stretch of the imagination. I knew it would be. While talking to friends about it, I knew it was going to be vicious no matter who the Democratic nominee would be. But one thing I noticed early on in 2008, 2010, 2012, and 2014 is the Democrats lost the midterm elections with Chairwoman of the DNC, Debbie Wasserman Shultz, at the helm, and the DNC kept her there. Then in 2016, we lost seats again and the Presidency. Did we not notice a pattern at this point? I did.

Shultz either was not working hard to keep Democrats in their local seats or the Republicans were so smart they just overshadowed whatever Debbie was doing. Democrats lost more seats in 2014 than ever before. The chairwoman was also a Senator with personal health issues (as she stated) who was trying to do two jobs and raise a family.

I remember listening to one of my favorite talk show hosts on WCPT, and the topic in 2010 was the loss of seats to Republicans in the House. He was angry because he thought the Dems did a horrible job in defending their House seats. After President Barack Obama had won his second term, Mitch McConnell and the boys decided on a new strategy to gain the WH back. But the radio host was not happy with the Democratic Party and railed against their strategy. The GOP needed to run someone who was a trash talker, big baller, and had their sights set on winning at all costs—even if it meant allowing Russian President Vladimir Putin to influence or sway our voting population any way he could.

In part, it meant using Julian Assange's ability to access unauthorized emails by the Russians and give No. 45 all the talking points he needed to sprinkle doubt into the minds of voters. I wouldn't be surprised if people in the audience at some of No. 45's rallies were paid Russian guests. So, let me get into the meat of what I believe happened and what is still happening because, apparently, we have blinders on at this point.

Let me end my introduction with this: when Barack Obama, then candidate Obama, ran against Senator John McCain, of course I wanted Obama to win the election in 2008. It was an exciting time. At the time, I had developed a slipped disc in my back, and for most of that year, I was off work at home. My husband and I were watching the news and any comments, statements, events which had anything to do with candidate Obama. We even managed to attend a rally in Norfolk Virginia with family, and it was awesome.

But let me say this, Senator John McCain took the microphone away from a woman in the audience who wanted to ask a question when she stated she thought Barack Obama was an Arab (it was so sad and funny at the same time) and Senator McCain responded to her by reaching for her microphone saying this, "no miss, no miss, no, he is a good family man that I happen to have disagreements with on policy." I knew, without hesitation, that Senator McCain was an honorable man at that moment. Then when Donald J. Trump (I refuse to use his name for this book more than 3 or 4 times) said he likes people who weren't captured, I knew we were facing a scummy, nasty, pathetic little man.

I thought to myself what in the world happened to this person along the way in his life that would make him say that about a man who sacrificed his life for his country? I asked myself, what kind of man or person is this? I know people that served in the military and I would never disparage the sacrifice they make. What dark cloud has been in this person's life that would make him fix his mouth to say something like that? This is not just a smart-mouthed person making a life out of people. Something is awry somewhere. The pieces aren't fitting together.

Chapter One

*****

What The Hell Happened?

Right off the bat, who told the Democratic National Committee to run five people? With all the talented politician's they have in their party, they found five people to run. Namely Hillary Rodham Clinton, Martin O'Malley of Baltimore, Vermont Senator Bernie Sanders (I), former Senator of Virginia Jim Webb, and Rhode Island's former governor, Lincoln Chafee. I can think of at least 20 senators, former Democratic governors, or former House members that could have run for the job. Even if they didn't want the job—they could have stood there like the 17 Republicans did knowing they weren't getting that job. I think only two people thought they were getting the job of President: No. 45 and Ted Cruz.

There should never be another time in our history in which the Democrats run five people. Also, there should never be any

Democratic candidates that stand there and tear each other down. Their job is to talk to the camera and talk about the horrible job that Republicans are doing from start to finish. There is no time or break in the conversation to talk about the other candidate in the same party. All eyes should be on Republicans and how they're tearing this country down from limb-to-limb.

Just this week (on March 6, 2017), six Democrats voted to confirm Ben Carson for the top job of HUD. Knowing that he is going to gut the Department of Housing and Urban Development, yet the Dems voted to confirm him. Whenever Dems need votes from Republicans, they get two. Are we gullible or just plain oblivious? Is the new chairman of the DNC going to reign in his members or just let them continue to go rogue? When No. 45 gave his first speech, there was not one Dem that came out afterward and gave a rebuttal. I was floored when no one had anything to say after this new President said all the horrible things he said about Mexicans.

No. 45 talked about how the African-Americans have nothing to lose by voting for him. His rallies were full of violence, he read stolen emails, and not one Democrat could find anything to say. He stated that he could grab women by the p***y and they let him do it. He nicknamed Senator Warren during the campaign 'Pocahontas,' and there was no rebuttal from the Democrats. He told the American people that Mexico was paying for the wall and now we are expected to pay? His first bill was to put a tax on first-time home buyers, and there was nothing to be said? He has Steve Bannon working for him, a known racist in the White House as the Chief Strategist, and there was nothing to say—nothing to rebut? Really?

A terrible mistake that I believe was made is that candidate Secretary Hillary Rodham Clinton seemed to wander out haphazardly about her intent to run while allowing Vt. Senator Bernie Sanders gain a lot of momentum with voters. She allowed this man who virtually no one knew to get a tremendous head-start.

But I knew him because of his "Friday with Bernie" show on WCPT Radio with Thom Hartmann. I listened to him most Fridays, and he gave answers to the major issues facing America. He never gave solutions. I didn't personally see him saying, "What we should do is this and that," as having a winning strategy to help your party. But, as we know now, Bernie Sanders did not give answers for the Democrats to resolve. In my view, he gave directives—every Friday.

I have followed politics and race relations in policy since I was in eighth-grade. I started from the murder of President John F. Kennedy by a paid sniper to the killing of Dr. Martin L. King in Memphis Tennessee, up to the murder of Robert Kennedy. I have followed the evils that permeate our politics and they have continued "taking advantage" of Americans voters. I have followed what I believe is the culpability of the United States government who supported and encouraged slavery for over one hundred years and have not yet tried to restore those people to a philanthropic place in American society. It's shameful and unresolved!

The Senate and Congress will allow a political candidate who wants to run for the highest office in the country to hold his taxes when another President Barack Obama had to show his birth certificate just to shut up the noise and confusion. Why are we being made to pay taxes on April 15th? Does that make any sense to you? It doesn't, and No. 45 should show his taxes immediately. Mitch and the boys should demand him to show them.

There is nothing worse than having someone in the WH that is as much as a liar than what we see in kid's cartoons like 'Pinocchio,' who's big fat nose is getting longer and longer. During the campaign, I was shocked to see all these people who were just charmed by this man. They were smitten on him. I had seen Trump for years and years. He would host pageants on television. He would show up on late night television shows. I used to listen to him on the Howard Stern Show when Stern was on terrestrial radio—before he went to satellite. That's when No. 45 did most of his best shtick, lingo, and mere talk. One of the biggest stories I remember is when he was messing around with Marla Maples. It was scandalous. He was always a player, and he wasn't ashamed of that title. You could tell he was the biggest bull-shitter on the planet, by design.

He never wanted to run for President because he knew he didn't have the education or background. He's a real estate developer who didn't go to college to study law. He felt inferior until one of his archenemies got the job—a black man from Chicago that went to Harvard law school with a name like Obama. This was a 65-year-old man with ideas and thoughts from his father who told him they don't rent to blacks. He came up at a time when black people were struggling to find their way in America and make this place better for them overall. Number 45 came up when white people were still in the height of keeping their foot on the neck of black folks. That's what he and his father were about—oppression.

Then came the icing on the cake that would make his friends cringe. At the 2014 press dinner, President Obama did the unthinkable. He made fun of and made the whole room laugh at No. 45 and his outrageous birther idea. In other words, he was being made to look like a fool. But No. 45 had done that all by himself when he claimed that President Obama was not born in the United States. I could see Governor Rick Scott of Florida look around at another guest to see how badly No. 45 was taking the jokes. I think Governor Rick Scott knew at the time. "I see smoke coming off the top of his hair." By then, this New York real estate developer went back to his lofty office in Trump Tower and cried on the shoulder of anyone who would listen.

And the worst of the worst did listen to him complain, and he promised retaliation. His 'listeners' took advantage of the fact that No. 45 wanted to get back at his foes. They knew about his spiteful and revengeful demeanor. These are friends that realize this man will go off half-cocked if you tell him something. In other words, No. 45 will say what others want to say, but doesn't have the guts to do anything. He would not sleep restfully until he did anything and everything he could to make President Obama look bad and put the Democrats to rest.

This campaign was as if there was a war room created to fight Hillary Clinton, and she would not get elected if the Russians had anything to say about it. So, they fed No. 45 or his minions information and the team of Reince Priebus and Sean Spicer told them to always be on the offense. They were told to make sure when you go on the talk shows or you're being asked to do an interview, that it's not about No. 45, that it's against Hillary Clinton. They never discussed Vt. Senator Bernie Sanders or said anything negative about him, unless it was to build a wall between Sanders and Clinton. It was always facts and negatives about Hillary Clinton.

According to, MSNBC's reporting, after No. 45 was elected, he seemed to know too much for a New York Real Estate Developer (who had virtually no experience) to gain the WH without a lick of experience. He was a person that had no connection to politics— except possible information coming from former Mayor of New York, Rudy Giuliani, and Governor Chris Christie. But Christie has his own set of problems in New Jersey. But Christie wanted to get the hell out of dodge and decided to run for President of the United States himself. It appears someone from inside the WH on the Republican side was feeding information to the campaign of No. 45.

For a New York Real Estate Developer No. 45 knew too much!

It appears that someone from the Russian side who knew political facts about Clinton and those damn emails was feeding the information to Trump Tower. The Republicans picked three of Clinton's negatives and stuck to those three facts; Bill Clinton's infidelity and impeachment, the Benghazi debacle, and her private email server.

I should say that the news programs that I paid more attention to are mainstream news like NPR, PBS, WCPT, MSNBC, CNN and I trust them. As far as publications go I read: The Nation, The Guardian, Politico, Huffington Post, The Chicago Tribune, Washington Post, Wall Street Journal, The Atlantic, The New Yorker, and those are publications again that I trust. The only one that I did not watch equally is FOX News—especially after it came out that Roger Ailes was being accused of sexual harassment. I feel it's just not a reputable station and they dogged President Obama the whole time he was in office for no other reason than race. So, if a television station shows bias when it's not even necessary—in other words, if President Obama had a questionable past or reckless way in which he ran the office—then they may have a point. But it was pure unsaturated race-baiting and racially biased news reporting at that television station in my opinion.

Finally, this is my opinion, and I wanted to place and cite some of the information that I came across about various subjects and/or people inside the book. This election has caused me to speak out against an attack on our First Amendment rights and against Russia sticking their nose into our elections. I am livid about how this all went down over the 18-months of campaigning; as I learn more and more from news reports, and experts, and not limited to historians. CNN has done a good job of giving us history lessons about Putin and his hatred for Hillary Rodham Clinton. I think the Kremlin's attack against our highly respected electoral process; which many countries would love to have despite its faults, was treated disrespectfully, and with impertinence to the highest degree.

Chapter Two

*****

The Republican War Room

The Republicans pulled out all the stops in this election. They were determined not to allow the Supreme Court to turn liberal or all of America's ills would be lost. For example, their treaties with Indians would continue to stand. Right now, they may be at risk. Look at what's happening at Standing Rock in North Dakota. The 1964 Voting Rights Act hangs in the balance—even though No. 45 said he would do this or that for black folks. I wasn't listening to it. The issue of gun control was twisted and used to scare white people into believing, if you're not armed—they're coming to get you. The abortion rights would be turned on its head, and Planned Parenthood would run amuck with killing babies. And unless we build a wall to keep Mexicans out, our jobs will never return. He kept saying, "A big beautiful wall with a big door." He is right a big door where our taxes will fly right out of that big beautiful wall.

They knew if Hillary Rodham Clinton won the American election, white women and the feminist movement would put white men in the basket of 'nowhere to go." The election for No. 45 was done by making Mexicans feel like because of them being here—we aren't working, and it's their fault. No. 45 used black preachers to go into their churches and make a pitch that if they vote for him; he would be their 'great white hope.' Black preachers from the Red States and Ohio; promoted votes for No. 45 more than he does for God. I just wonder how many jobs were produced, or factories built, or construction jobs created in those poor cities? Been there—heard that before.

Ronald Reagan was the worse divider-in-chief that was ever elected. He slashed all types of programs—especially for mental illness, the poor, education, yet he sold arms to Iran. That was Reagan's biggest failure, and it has consequences today. Lt. Oliver North and Reagan sold arms to Iran, the country that they rail against today as the bogey man. The weapons they use against Americans; were probably sold to them by the Republicans under Donald Rumsfeld to Iran in the seventies. In his later years, Reagan was not coherent enough to run that office. His staff and vice president had to take over most of his duties.

When the Republicans lost that election in 2008, they had allowed the banks to run rough shot over the banking industry and mess homeowners up in the meantime to where they lost their homes and jobs. It didn't start with the 2008 crash. It started with Enron and that whole crazy debacle and disaster. But the homeowners forgot how that felt. They forgot about the financial meltdown. They put their faith right back into the hands of the ones who bit them only eight years ago? Did they forget how their payments ballooned up so high, did they forget that they lost money in their IRAs. What would make them vote for Republicans ever again? Fear. The gun control advocates make them vote on fear. It works every time. They take the money from memberships for the NRA and give it to politicians to vote their way in Congress. The NRA and Russia own the Republican Senate. After what happened to the children at Sandyhook Elementary School, I bet most of the people in that town voted for No. 45. It's probably the sad truth.

This bunch is heartless and reckless, just as Joe McCarthy deemed the Congress as having many communists. He suffered the consequences of those charges. McCarthy devised a blacklist of people he believed were Communist. He believed during the Cold War that the House of Representatives were infiltrated with communist. It makes you wonder if McCarthy was on to something. McCarthy suffered being ostracized for taking a stand like that against his Republican colleagues. Before it was all said and done, they avoided him and left the room when he entered. They said he was hurt and disappointed that his peers ignored him. He believed that premise. It is something patently wrong with our congressmen today.

There is a cult-like fear on the structure of the Republican Party. Why do they always vote the same way? Why is there no independent thinkers among them and if so, why don't they speak out? Even when Senator Lindsey Graham and his friend Senator John McCain try to speak up about missteps they are pulled right back in by someone or something. They say Congressman don't want to be Cantered; I think they don't want to be McCarthy-ized.

The Republicans may not all be communist, but something is awry in that party, and over the past 40 years, it seemingly got worse. The GOP Party is not embarrassed to say how lopsided they've become towards other races. However, when the Southern States dominate the voting patterns and the hateful attitudes that come from that part of the country—then you must consider the mindset of the people that govern from there. They are not only the older stauncher racist patterns in language and theme has certainly simmered over into the younger candidates as well. These white-haired old guards from the most racist cities in America are now running amuck in Congress. They do it with the healthcare bill, and I knew that when No. 45 said he would give you a beautiful healthcare plan—it was all bullshit.

President Obama went on the campaign trail during the 2016 election to warn voters about this horrific person that ran for the Republican Party, who was rich and ornery and did not have your well-being in mind. But the voters were hell-bent on voting for the slick New York businessman. If you chose any corporation around the country… just pick one, have they ever been concerned about their worker or their bottom line? Don't these corporations pay low wages but when they retire they get a massive retirement package? How do you think they gain those increases? They do it off your backs. You do the hard work, and they get rewarded. It's simple. For the life of me, I don't understand why that premise wasn't concerned when everybody was so smitten with No. 45. Duh!

The insurance companies are no different. They want to be able to charge whatever prices they want. Although, we can go to places like India, Mexico, Canada, or Taiwan and get healthcare at a rate unlike the 'billionaire healthcare' that most people in America can't afford. They want to be able to banish poor people of the roles. Why? Because you're poor, and it benefits them not one iota; to give you all their proper health care diagnosis in the long run. You are not going to get half of all the promises that were made to you on the campaign trail. As a matter of fact, by the summer this man won't come to your State to see you or talk to you about his decisions. That is over, done, finished!

Like I mentioned the Republicans had to come up with a gimmick to get elected. They had the gimmicks of Vladimir Putin's ex KGB operative, now President of Russia, and very knowledgeable about how and what needed to be done to get his candidate of choice elected. The Clinton email server began three years before the actual 2016 election. Like Mike McCarthy said, "it was our goal to bring her numbers down, and that has happened." Senator Mitch

McConnell and the boys decided just to keep quiet and pay attention to elections in their own district. His plan was not to make any statements that might lead to the loud-mouth New Yorker to get thrown off the ticket. He was doing a hatchet job on the other Republican's and McConnell, and the boys stood by and laughed while No. 45 gave it to them. Behind the scenes and in the rooms of the Capitol building—they all laughed. The sneaky look on the face of Congressman Paul Ryan you see today is the same smirk he had when his boss told him just to keep cool and not comment about the foul-mouthed New Yorker.

As I was writing a few weeks ago, No. 45 accused President Barack Obama of wiretapping Trump Tower. The Republican's go around and chuckle and giggling like Speaker of the House did today when asked about whether he thought the accusations are true. This Speaker Ryan acts like he's 15-years-old boy. He constantly giggles, smirks or snorts his way through these very national questions. Not only was President Obama continually besmirched by these white guys in the WH and outside, but they also hate his approval ratings are at 62% as he left the office. Donald Trump looks at television and sees this slim, polished lawyer, intelligent, handsome brother with a wonderful family, a smart wife that an attorney; and No. 45 goes whack-a-doodle.

The same thing happened to Glenn Beck and Lou Dobbs, which led them to get fired from NBC; they started making unreasonable statements and putting up chalkboards, and charts. What a hot mess!

Those two gentlemen lost it. You could literally see them become unraveled during their television shows. It took a long time for the executive producers to catch on, but the world saw them lose it.

Chapter Three

*****

Whack-a-do's Everywhere

During the entire campaign of 2016, there seemed to be supporters of No. 45 that mentally seemed to be in a trace or fog. The numbers of supporters at rallies that resorted to violence was unprecedented. The guest that showed up on various television shows talked fast and hurried, and never stuck to the question. They would flip the question they were asked and dodge the answer by talking about HRC. It appeared that before these people entered the room, they were given a pill that made them forget who they were supporting for the President of the United States.

The person they were promoting had a dreadful background of leaving contractors unpaid, borrowing millions from Deutsche Bank and not paying it back, and denigrating Mexicans and a New York

Mexican judge. He has business ties with Russian oligarchs and a former KGB Agents. He was caught playing around on his wife with another woman; he was divorced two times, he made comments about women that resembled sexual assault.

These whack-a-dos continued their daily, nightly, weekly, and monthly rants about HRC, and totally forgot about the lawsuit against minorities he and his father was served for housing discrimination. They totally compared these charges against the email server issue as reported by Julian Assange (WikiLeaks) a known rapist that was extradited from Sweden for his dirty deeds. It's amazing and dumbfounding that we followed a man that was expelled from his own country for being accused of rape--if it wasn't true. Why is he hiding out in Ecuador? WikiLeaks is a resource for information, but the man behind the leaks is similar with any thug in the street.

Because Americans know little about history and politics, and conflicts we have between different countries, voters had no clue about Putin's hate and disdain for Hillary Clinton. As a candidate in 2007, she said, "Putin doesn't have a soul." From that point on he hated HRC—forever. Even former U.S. Secretary of Defense Robert F. Gates is convinced that Vladimir Putin targeted our election in 2016. Particularly the Putin operatives went after HRC and DNC which was going to help No. 45 win and HRC lost. It was one of the most surprising losses of our time. With the help of Vladimir Putin sticking his influence in on our election, it changed—in my view—

our democracy...forever. Now since being in office less than 30 days, No. 45 has a failed military operation that will follow him as did Benghazi for HRC.

This is from NPR Online February 27, 2017

"I told them I didn't want to make a scene about it, but my conscience wouldn't let me talk to him," Owens said of the president in an interview with **The Miami Herald**. He made that decision after being told that Trump was heading from Washington to attend the transfer of Ryan Owens' remains.

The Navy SEAL died on Jan. 29, in a rare ground mission in Yemen. Since then, the U.S. has acknowledged that more than 20 civilians, including women and children, **were also killed in the attack**, along with 14 al-Qaida militants. Almost immediately after the raid, questions were also raised about whether the gains of the raid were enough to offset the loss of an elite U.S. special operator and an Osprey aircraft.

The White House has deemed the mission a success, despite the losses and the apparent escape of one of the raid's key targets. From **NPR's fact check** that included Pentagon correspondent Tom Bowman:

"But the U.S. would not send in SEAL Team Six, the premiere anti-terrorist commandos, to pick up some cell phones and computers, a U.S. official told Bowman.

"Part of the effort was to get top al-Qaida in the Arabian Peninsula, or AQAP, leaders. While more than a dozen militants were killed, a top target, Qassim al-Rimi, either slipped away or was not at the location."

Discussing the raid, William Owens, who is also a military veteran, told the *Miami Herald*, "Why at this time did there have to be this stupid mission when it wasn't even barely a week into his administration? Why? For two years prior, there were no boots on the ground in Yemen — everything was missiles and drones — because there was not a target worth one American life. Now, all of a sudden we had to make this grand display?"

I don't want to hear any more gobbledygook about Benghazi from No. 45 and his administration. Because if you don't care about Gold Star parents, then you are feckless and just have no heart or sense of what it means. It is apparent that No. 45 is so anxious to make himself as famous as President Barack Obama (which will never, ever, never happen) he made a horrific huge mistake to sign off on this military mission. The new administration tried to blame him for this mission and say it was ordered before Obama left. Another lie and epic fail.

It's amazing that No. 45 and his minions beat HRC over the head about a failed military mission and as you can see No. 45 is no magician when it comes to ordering an incident free military mission. Michael Flynn, Steve King, Jeff Sessions (U.S. Senator) and No. 45 chanted, "Lock her up" for it. Michael Flynn was not reciting the same chants, yet he did not sign up as a foreign agent—before the 2016 campaign. What a pathetic person. While Flynn had the nerve to get rally goers chanting "lock her up" he was reportedly making his money, the payoff of $500,000 (half-a-million) dollars while chanting insults about someone who is not a foreign agent. There is no shame with these people. As a matter of fact, it's best we don't hear lies and excuses from Michael Flynn ever again.

The President keeps saying that Obamacare is a disaster. People that have the ACA, Affordable Care Act don't feel that way. People are too afraid to even say they have the coverage. There's an element of secrecy that hides behind signing up for ACA. If you need healthcare and you get a subsidy to help pay for your coverage, why is that shameful? I suppose because the friends of these people talked about it so badly that you should be embarrassed about using the ACA. By the way, the ACA and Obamacare are the same.

There is not a separate health care program by the name of Obamacare and another called ACA. I think people were fooled into believing it was different. Like Obamacare is for the poor, down-and- out class, for minorities and the ACA was developed for the high and mighty. It's just not true. We must enlighten ourselves and read more.

The man in the WH during the campaign was screaming and yelling about Obamacare like it was an alien baby or something.

Another crazy scheme that Republicans are trying to sell is we should pay for a wall that half of us don't give a damn about, which would cost billions of dollars. I say if the rich want it—then pay for it. They're not paying any taxes, and they can afford to build the wall. If the border patrol was doing a good job, why do we need a wall? You can't make somebody pay for something they didn't order. Have you ever received something you didn't order? What is your normal response? "I didn't order that. I'm not paying for that!" And that's what America should say as well.

Taxpayers should not pay for any wall when the country is in a healthcare crisis. The reason Republicans hate Obamacare is they don't like his name. They want to erase the memory of this man. They don't want President Obama to have any successes.

We also should not pay for a wall when our infrastructure is failing. Another thing, what about dealing with the jobs he promised. I know the white working class in Ohio, Michigan, Wisconsin, and Pennsylvania are waiting for those factories that No. 45 said he would re-open again to open again. Isn't that what all this was about? I bet the people in the Red States who put their political banks on the line must be waiting in the wings for the mass burst of jobs to come back to make us great again.

Chapter Four

*****

Third-Party Messiness

This will probably be the shortest chapter in the book because being enthusiastic about three or four different parties is not my idea of running a solid campaign. I realize you can't stop people from running in the campaign, but the Independent who became a Democrat did not work for me and here's why.

Being involved in a political party takes work, work, and more work. What you cannot do is be introverted when you decide to become a politician. It involves attending meetings when you don't want to. Talking to people you may know are not on your side. It takes talking to the opposition and trying to agree on a path that you know you will never reach— together. It means listening to people who are 'arm-chair' politicians. In other words, they seemingly don't know how politics works. You meet with civic leaders who are against you and don't want you to win. I said earlier in my book that I knew of---Senator Bernie Sanders.

The way that I came to know him is from listening to him on WCPT on Friday's on his "Lunch with Bernie Show." It was interesting. I knew Sanders was an Independent in the Senate. What I did not know is his feelings about Black Lives Matters, which I don't remember him bringing up during his radio show. I did not know that he marched for fair housing in Chicago. He never talked about that on his show. What I noticed is he stopped appearing on his show, and the next thing I knew he was running for President of the United States. He did a good job of coming out of the starting gates and making a huge splash at the rallies.

I think also Senator Sanders knew that something was different about this election. He was aware that there was a lot of negativity coming toward his opponent Hillary Clinton yet he did very little to defend her or the Democratic Party. He talked more about what he wanted to do for the country. I personally saw his interference, as a way, to stop HRC from winning. And bigger than this was two men who were daring a female to run for President of the United States. Hillary made her series of mishaps along the way, and so did the

DNC and its members in general. I will get to that later in the book.

The independents wanted to be heard, and for years they had not been listened to. Independents like Ed Schultz, Bernie Sanders, Thom Hartmann, Stephanie Miller, and Alan Combs (who I miss so much since he died) added so much to enlighten the conversation. They had very good ideas and synergy to the conversation overall. Mr. Combs was humorous, smart, patient and provided an intelligent induction for WCPT radio. I looked forward to listening to his opinion on the days' politics every night until his voice was stilled because of his passing. He will be missed.

Chapter Five

*****

How Media is Bias

As I said, I watched all news stories and grew to know many hosts like; Paul Pacalia, Van Jones, Anna Navarro, David Axelrod (whom I knew about from Chicago politics). As reported by *OPINION* online, March 15, 2017, cited thirteen surrogates that appeared on various shows like CNN or MSNBC and FOX to defend No. 45 served as dutiful attack dogs. So much so, the host of various shows couldn't keep up and had no comeback answers when they steadily attacked Hillary Clinton.

People like Rudy Giuliani, Mike Flynn, Kayleigh McEnany, Michael Cohen, Al Baldasaro, Corey Lewandowski, Boris Epshteyn, Kellyann Conway, Steve Miller, Scottie Hughes, Omarosa Stallworth, Kevin Burns, Katrina Pierson, Bruce Levell, and Darrell

Scott a Cleveland pastor were on the television nightly for 18-months. If they weren't on television, they were Tweeting habitually against Hillary Clinton and President Obama.

With that said the media on all of the television stations particularly MSNBC, CNN, and FOX gets an F- an epic failure and if there was a grade lower than that I would administer it. They should get the worse grade because the reporting was not even and not investigative like it was when President Obama ran. When President Obama ran in 2008, you had reporters travel to Kenya for stories. They got in the face of his Auntie. Reporters traveled to The University of Chicago, Harvard University, interviewed childhood friends and foes.

Reporters sought out teachers, his sister, his brothers from Kenya. They did stories on Michelle Obama's parents her brother and her family's background. They sent reporters to his church Trinity on the Southside of Chicago to interview and listen to Reverend Wright's sermons. The media took his books *Dreams of My Father* and deciphered them and put them through a laser beam of scrutiny like you wouldn't believe. Media did an expose 'about President Obama's grandmother and grandfather in Kansas and what their jobs had been. They did an interview with his publishers and anyone who had anything to do with the book.

Certain television shows had shown bias and predisposition toward President Obama before he opened his mouth. They were gleeful when his budget or opposition was on the horizon it seemed. Reporters like Jake Taper from CNN, who has been recently banned from the media press corp. Since No. 45 was elected, he is not sitting in the front seat asking questions any longer.

I remember President Obama saying to Taper, "You ought to know better," about something he said about the president. Host, Anderson Cooper tries to be fair and not show bias during his reporting on CNN. He tries very hard to keep it neutral—even when he interviewed No. 45 during the campaign.

But of all the things I named you did not see this when No. 45 ran for office. What church did they visit? Did they talk to friends of the Trump family? Did they go back to the neighborhoods where he lived before he moved to Manhattan? We know very little about his grandparents. Did media do an expose' on his heritage as they did for President Obama? Did media go through his books cover-to-cover to see if there was a hidden message about doing in the country? Where was the follow-up about the "birther" scheme by media? Did media go to Kenya to see if No. 45 had sent investigators there and did anyone speak to them? I never saw a sit-down interview by media with No. 45s sister, who is a judge in New York City.

The entire time during the 2016 campaign, there seemed to be biased reporting. It wasn't even, and it was not investigative in nature. It was talking heads dressed up nicely asking surrogates questions and basically allowing them to take over the one-hour shows. Where were the notes of previous things they said, perhaps the night before? There was no fact checking going on. The media had six surrogates for Hillary Clinton; Robby Mook, Amy Weinshoussen, Kevin Bailey, David Axelrod, James Carville and um can't remember anybody else.

I can't name ten surrogates that came out nightly in favor for HRC. Her daughter is ineffective as a spokesperson for her mother. She sounded weak and frail in her support for her "mom." It was clearly noticeable that HRC was terrified of coming to the podium to speak up for herself or hold a press conference in fear of being asked about Benghazi. After about the fifth time she answered the email and Benghazi question no more answers should have been given on the subject. How many times can you answer that question? Yet, the media hounded and pounded that question in the ground. But I haven't heard those same questions given to No. 45 about Navy Seal Owens death in Yemen.

Once the media figured out they could make money from No. 45, his rallies and appearances were where they were focused. They ran to every one of his rallies. They interviewed his surrogates before, during, and after the rallies. The media made sure they covered the rally word-for-word.

There was no outrage by media when candidate No. 45 kicked out a Mexican journalist for asking questions at a press conference. No. 45 ordered a reporter from UNIVISION to leave the room and not participate in the news conference. He has yet to be invited back. I saw one of the Secret Service members escort him out of the hotel ballroom. Shameful!

When candidate No. 45 came down the golden escalator and read a statement about Mexicans why didn't MSNBC, CNN, NPR, PBS, and all the other news outlets do stories on the contributions made to this country? He should dispel the outrageous things being said about them. There were no investigative reports done to compare violence perpetrated by Mexicans v. the same crime committed by other nationalities. Where was the report on that? Day-after-day the media let those reports stand in the open. Ironic!

Even up until now, after President Obama is gone—out of office and the media handled it horribly—about wiretapping. I knew it was bullshit and why doesn't media call it for what it is? I suppose they can't or won't. I guess that's why some of us are not a journalist. How do they keep their composure? I was watching Sean Spicer at this so-called press briefs, where he gets to read a dissertation of fake news to the reporters that are there to gather the news. It's just dumb and unacceptable. Let me tell you the playbook.

When dictators want to control votes and the "world" what do they do first? They should streamline the opposition first. They hire people that are siding with them and fire everyone else. Over a short period of time, this can be accomplished. The media is suppressed by not telling them who is coming to visit the President and what did they discuss. That could be the media, or it could be government organizations like the Department of State, Department of Education, Department of Agriculture, Depart of Housing and Urban Development. So, these and other organizations are being stripped financially. They will be dysfunctional and out of operation. Even 'meals on wheels,' is going to be decimated. Block grants to beautify the neighborhood or a community center will be destroyed. In other words, we ladies and gentlemen will have no government.

Like I said to me this is nothing more than a coup d'état' of our government's computer system. Of course, it could not be done militarily—it's too obvious to the public—they can't afford a national uprising. It will be done quietly, methodically, and defensively—with no opposition. Why is the media not talking more about paranoia schizophrenia and what it does to people? They can do an expose' on paranoia schizophrenia and what seemingly is happening in the WH. Just do some investigating like they did when President Obama was in office.

Could it be that someone we know is suffering from mental illness? It appears that we have on our hands a person that believes the former President would wiretap him. What a crazy idea for anyone to come up with. He has the belief that everyone is out to get him. I wonder why? It's preposterous!

Russia has a communist regime, but it was more open and democratic leaning when Boris Yeltsin was there. The first president of the Russian Federation before Vladimir Putin was Boris Yeltsin, who served from 1991 to late 1999. Mr. Putin then became president for two terms from 2000 to 2008. Dmitry Medvedev became president from 2008 to 2012, until Mr. Putin came into office as president again from 2012 onwards.

Let me get back to the lack of reporting about No. 45's heritage and history. They didn't try to do an investigative report on No. 45 or his campaign helpers. Called "helpers" instead of surrogates is what I will call them. The media did a piss-poor job of investigating them. Proof is back in September Michael Flynn a retired military conspiracy theorist was working inside Russia and getting paid as a Foreign Agent while he was helping Donald J. Trump called out HRC for giving speeches with Goldman Saks executives. Now, which is worse? Getting paid to be a Foreign Agent while a retired military general or getting paid for a speech in the USA by a well-known bank. You tell me.

The tawdry theme that Michael Flynn kept up was her private email server hidden in her basement. "The bogeyman!" If the State

Department didn't make a big deal out of it--why would I as a voter? HRC mentioned that others were doing it too. But the female running for President of the United States was vilified and ostracized for having a private server. Why not say we don't want a person that is in opposition to Vladimir Putin in office. We as voters, though, rode that horse all the way to the finish line and look what we found at the end of it. Someone that hasn't told us the truth—never, ever! This is someone who won't show their taxes and never will show them. Why? In my view, they obviously have a lot to hide. The response that No. 45 gives speaks for itself.

The media must do an unbiased job of reporting. If you do a rich expose of one President during his campaign, then the public expects you to do the same reporting on the next Presidential candidate. Go to his neighborhood, speak to his friends, go to his church, speak to his pastor, and use a type of his pastor's beliefs within the church. Reports should have spoken with his sisters and brothers, people who met him at business meetings. None of that was done. And if it was, there were no follow-up questions. It was seemingly easier to make it look like President Obama was an alien that plopped down from the sky and invaded America.

The Democrats have an arsenal of negative press to use against No. 45. Which the new head of the DNC Tom Perez should be exposing every time he speaks. I saw him on Chris Hayes a few nights ago, and he was talking gibberish and gobbledygook. It was totally irrelevant to the subject matter of Obamacare. Again, the messaging is just horrible. I could do what Perez did in two seconds.

"Chris, we have a killer healthcare plan put forth by No. 45 and the Republicans that will expel 24,000,000 women and children and seniors from the healthcare roles. The plan Republicans supporting my friends are a death panel if I ever saw one. They keep saying that Obamacare is bad and it only has 11,000,000 people on the roles. Why? Because their caucus never funded Obamacare and they never wanted to fund Obamacare. Can it be improved yes it can?

Speaker of the House Paul Ryan is their hatchet man. He wants to kick millions of women and children off the roles. If you want to do something for the vulnerable 30% of the country in regards to healthcare—fund it. And the seniors will have to pay 30% more towards their healthcare. All this is a rouse. This is a shell game and baits and switch. No. 45 said he wanted everybody to have healthcare. This healthcare proposal doesn't do that. But they only want to help the top 1% of this country to be able to buy healthcare and other people vulnerable that are currently on the ACA already will be kicked off like a dog in the night." Sad!

Lastly, why don't Democrats talk to people who have ACA? It's easy to find people who have it and can tell them what it's like going to a doctor's office with the ACA card in their hand. First, the card does not say "Obamacare Healthcare Card," it will have your healthcare provider on it. You can't intelligently speak about something you have no experience with. Republicans are telling people they are tired of funding the poor. Wow! What a statement. In other words, "we rather see you sick on the streets without Section 8 and pay for a wall than to pay for your healthcare." The sick and the poor can go to hell. That's what Republicans have said. It doesn't get any clearer than that.

Chapter Six

*****

What the Democrats Must Change

I have been following Democratic politics for a very, very long time. I know some of the players in politics and remember them from Richard Nixon's time and Ronald Reagan. The GOP has built up Ronald Reagan as a deity. He was not. He came in office firing people. He fired the Air Traffic Controllers within the first month of him arriving in Washington. It was an out-an-out assault on Unions, and it has been going on within the Republican Party ever since. They do not benefit from you having a Union that will represent you in wages, healthcare benefits, and your off time including sick days, PTO and safety on the job. They rather not have regulations and send you down the shaft of the coalmine without OSHA having inspected the tunnels.

The Republicans keep saying that they have a unified Party and that is the only thing that is true about them. The feckless laws they want to pass, the poor that they want to put their foot on their necks, and their ability to spin what is a lie into something their constituents will buy is what they are super good at. The Democrats using spin not so much.

As a matter of fact, the Democrats suck at this. During the campaign which went on for 18-months only had four surrogates that I remember coming out to speak on Hillary's behalf. On the aircraft, she seemed unsure of herself and skeptical of questions media were asking. When you run against a person like No. 45—all bets are off. But she couldn't do that because HRC wanted to portray herself as a "nice" lady. When someone is attacking you like NO. 45 did to her, she should have gone for his jugular vein right in plain open sight.

One thing I have a huge problem with Democrats regarding messaging. All of them say different things when asked a question from a reporter. When asked what you think about Obamacare; one Senator might say, "It's a program that was created with a lot of concern for people who didn't have healthcare. It has taken America 40-years to come up with a healthcare plan." Instead of saying this, "Democrats for the first time has created a healthcare plan that has helped millions, does it need improvements yes.

But it is far better than the plan that Republicans have—which is a big fat nothing burger for healthcare!" But what happens is another Democratic leader will come out and said, "Well it was a plan we brought to bear. It is not working like we had thought it would. There have been some problems with the computer system." Why didn't the person say that the Republicans offered nothing and what they did offer was a big fat nothing burger! I think they must build a list of 20 surrogates and they should be schooled about what they should say when asked certain questions.

The surrogates for No. 45 said one thing about him and went right into attack and defense mode. It worked for them. No. 45's attack dogs stuck to the script and didn't allow the reporter to turn them from their attacks or their questions. Look back at the YouTube videos. They were experts at it. Plus, they used up all the time spinning and negatively talking about Hillary.

I wished I was on the Communications Board for the Democrats. I would choose 20 to 40 of them who should speak on behalf of the candidate. In my view, other Democratic politicians cannot speak unless they go to training in communications, including Congressman Chuck Schumer. It would go a long way. No one is good at attacking or getting their agenda across without allowing reporters to stop them and get them off message. Time and time again they did that to Democrats. They were all over the map, they were confused, and they had no quotes from No. 45 in their hand to rebut what he said on the campaign trail. They must do a better job.

Fake News

Let me break down the meaning of "fake" news. It means news you will not accept to believe. It is not fake news as in they don't know what they are reporting. The conservative news media, especially on FOX has done a good job of spinning the news to benefit conservatives. It's this channel, which has done a creative job of making it seem like what you are seeing is "fake," and your eyes are deceiving you. FOX has spun their web for a very long time. Occasionally I might watch Chris Wallace, but he did come on board the chute of reality after No. 45 won the election. He knew he would have to get serious about the news to deal with the outrageous lies that were coming from the mouths of the new WH Administration.

During the first debate, the media handled the 17 candidates for President well. But Trump took control of the format quickly. What was interesting is the Kelly went right into No. 45 with his calling women dogs, calling Rosie O'Donnell ugly and fat. Seemingly, No. 45 has little or no time for chubbiness. In my estimation, he let you know when he had no place in the WH for Governor Christ Christie, another feckless peon that No. 45 turned lose.

He used his information, and then he kicked him to the curb. Yet, Steve Bannon got a free ride on the Trump/Putin train. Why Bannon and not Chris Christie who has governors experience? Outstanding! A white nationalist is what they call Steve Bannon founder and Chief orchestrator of Breitbart News the (Chief WH Strategist) to No. 45.

Amazing! But they can't let Megan Kelly use her journalistic experience to question No. 45. Let's speak of Kelly Ann Conway; she wants to share the spotlight of news and information with WH Speaker Sean Spicer. They should make up their mind who is going to be the lead communicator. Kelly Ann Conway does a horrible job. Sean gets upset and lets the reporters get under his skin. He does seem like he would like to ride his podium into the audience (press pool) because he gets so frustrated, as is portrayed on SNL on weekends. Spicer is ill-mannered and ill-tempered. He gets short with reporters. Here's another person that doesn't have the temperament for the job.

If you notice No. 45 wants you to believe that the media is all bad and has not reported his Russian ties correctly. In other words, they're all lying, and I'm telling the truth. He wants people to believe that what they're seeing is not what they're seeing or hearing. I had known No. 45 before he became President, through media accounts of course. I for the life of me don't know how they thought this man would make a good Commander-in-Chief? What about him says that? When dictators do that they want to edge out legitimate news as "fake" news and five or ten years from now those media outlets won't have any legitimacy anymore. On the Apprentice, No. 45 sat on his thrown and ordered people to be fired—which he relished and enjoyed.

Digital Fake Information

This is 2017, news fake or not doesn't need to be disseminated via a newspaper anymore. We use the Internet and social media. During 2016, the online radio stations were bombing HRC with commercials. They were interrupting commercials to do a negative commercial about her. In the State of Virginia, Barbara Comstock had ad after ad, and I saw nothing for HRC. Occasionally, I saw a "soft-shoe" ad about her–full of fluff, as if she were a fifteen-year-old running for high school President.

Communications have changed since Jennifer Palmieri started her internship with Leon Panetta in the 1990s. As a matter of fact, we didn't have some of the social media outlets that are being utilized today—at all. The ads I heard online radio would run every 10 minutes to HRCs that ran every 2 to 3 hours on iTunes Radio. Roby Mook avoided Twitter and didn't begin putting messages on there until I kept saying where are your communications? He finally got a hint. It took him a long time while HRC was getting lamb-basted with ads.

My concern is when you use the old guard, the same old (not as in age) but the same individuals that you have seen in each campaign and they are reused and regurgitated—how is that useful? The digital outlet that we have today were not available 30 years ago. An upgrade is imminent.

The Russians put a lot of money in pockets of communication influencers. Facebook had people on there, calling HRC names, and calling for her to be jailed. These were all a bunch of bots who had nothing but time on their hands. They were paid by someone to sit on the Internet night and day and spin negative stories about her. Then Twitter had the same thing, a bunch of people that you knew did negative spin all day long and half the night too. The same bots were using Michael Flynn's words 'lock her up" in ads, and they ran those sound bites over-and-over again. The digital war was sacrilege against HRC and her husband's past.

Speaking of which, Bill Clinton runs his mouth way too much, and HRC seems to have no control of it and doesn't outwardly take control. During the 2016 election, she is timidly and passively allowing Bill to ruin her chances. He said that Obamacare didn't make any sense. He got into a pissing match with people from BLM (Black Lives Matter). The social media bots took those statements and ran up the flag pole with them and regurgitated them back out into the ether a million times a day. Bill's words were repeated by pundit's, commercial ads, radio ads, print ads, social media comments and television ads. This man is not fit to serve did not hurt No. 45's chances. Why? Because there were so many ads out in No. 45's favor.

If you did some research, you could learn who the owners were of the various news outlets, online radio outlets, mobile ads, Internet ads against HRC was noticeably bombing the digital airways.

Every time Bill Clinton said something it would circulate over the Internet over and over. Each time a feud was created between him and BLM, it would circulate over the Internet. It was hard to tell which fake digital information was doing the most damage to the HRC campaign. All's we know is it did irreversible damage.

Digital communications move so fast and with precision faster than your eyes can blink. If you don't have the right people at the head, the tail will not follow. I started out my career in keypunch making the holes in cards for the noisy computers to read. There isn't a computer that I am afraid of and can do my own troubleshooting as well. You need to have a "Pitbull" communicator speaking on your behalf and then have the bots go on social media and say the same things. They need to be scheduled on every network and radio station terrestrial and Internet radio. What is still confusing to most people is why the Democrats have so many different messages with fewer surrogates spinning on her behalf.

I saw an interview with Bernie Sanders and reporter Dana Bash (CNN) the other night. She wouldn't allow Bernie to finish his sentence. These are the interviews I am talking about. The Democrats go on a show to pursue their agenda to the American public. The Republican's go on interview shows to attack Democrats. Everyone already knows what the Democratic agenda and what it stands for. The American public can go to their website for that information. We don't need Bernie Sanders, or Chairman of the DNC to come on television or a radio show to tell us what they believe how the country should perform or we should believe they do this or that.

When Democrats go on these shows, let people know what the Republicans are not for and what they're doing to this country by way of trying to implement a Gestapo tactic regime signed onto by Vladimir Putin. People in Russia are starving because he takes the money for his own lavish lifestyle. Is that how you want America to become? Because in that type of regime---everybody is the same.

With the Republicans, I would begin with Richard Nixon who was impeached, move on to Ronald Reagan, who took part in the Iran-Contra affair with Lt. Oliver North, who is akin to Lt. Michael Flynn (a traitor). Reagan sold arms to Iran (whom they claim to hate so much) then on to George H. Bush and George W. Bush (unqualified). I don't care who it is—they are not your friends. The Democrats don't have to keep beating the drums about No. 45; just go to the GOP and see what it has stood for. Have the Republicans implemented jobs in the past 45 years? Have they provided healthcare for the 320 million Americans in the past 45 years? Have they made it possible for tax cuts for the middle class and poor in this country?

The Democrats should have no other goal, but to go to the heart of the Republican Party and *squeeezzzze!*

Chapter Seven

*****

Enough Racism, Bias, Prejudice to Go Around

Racism is a noose around America's neck, and it always will be there, no matter how long the American government ignores its history. A communist country and regimes like Russia or any adversarial country can take advantage the list of indecencies' that were taken by the American government.

The GOP Party and the United States government in general held on to the economic empowerment of slavery for a way too long. The U.S. took advantage of free work they could take away from slaves, who were forced to come here to their shores and was grossly mistreated, disrespected, and wronged—which is an understatement.

There were no laws in place in the late 1700's to protect slaves from being whipped to death, starved to death, chased with dogs, stripped of their heritage, sabotaged by leaders in the WH at the time, and publicly humiliated, stopped from being a productive part of this society, slaves were hung for public entertainment and the women were raped and you know the rest.

Slaves were not treated with respect nor dignity and no concern that they had families as well. Even as of today, a black man will be fired after one offense, but the same happens with his white counterpart, and he is given a chance after chance. Why? He has a wife and kids to take care of. The "boss" doesn't take into consideration that the black man has a family as well. Often, the one and only pay check coming into the house is helping wife, mom, kids, grandma, and maybe a sick Aunt or Uncle.

Slavery is the one big embarrassment and indignity that America must face. There were no reparations for the freed slaves; no, we're sorry we did that to you; no, let's at least give them free education for the first 2 to 4 years. But they were so afraid black people would become competitive— they weren't even afforded any resemblance of reportorial payment. No offer of something for the work which was underpaid and/or never paid at all to African-Americans in America who were descendants of slaves.

With that said, do you think that other countries see this and know that if America thought they were inferior, then when they come to America that is the reason why in which African Americans are then perceived by other races that immigrate to America.

Although we may have built the sidewalk they are walking on – there is no respect for our history. History always must be considered—otherwise, you are undermining your own existence. America cannot exist peacefully until [and] unless they make good on their slimy past of the torture of slavery. As a matter of fact, white America would like African-Americans, it seems to disappear, and the history will disappear with it. That is not going to happen.

It's about the presentation and how America presented us to the world for the world to see when they maimed black people—not only physically—but mentally as well. How would you like to be considered the pariah in a country that you were brought to through no fault of your own? I know black people have some issues when it comes to housing, health, drug addiction, and criminal past.

Have you asked yourselves—could that be because of their beginning and not so much what their story has become in America as of now. However, it's no worse than anyone else's and what goes on in their countries. People ought not to point fingers.

And I'm not saying that black people have not had some successes, but it's so very far and few between when you look at our white counterparts and the jobs they are able to obtain. The jewelry business, furniture businesses, owning a shopping mall, buyer for department stores like Macy's, or owning a gas station. Where are black people in these boardrooms all over America? Why am I not seeing black men in the boardrooms of these large companies? You can see the deficiencies very plainly.

Why would people who have worked here, built the WH and contributed so much to this place should experience the drama and go through the hassle they do to vote in America. I remember I went to a protest in downtown Chicago a few years ago and my sign said, "We were brought here, and we built it too!" It's the truth. African Americans should be given a break-all-rules card. A "go" card that allows them to vote—period. If they are not breaking any laws—then give them a green "go" card, so they don't have to experience the humiliation and degradation of walking up to the table and being turned away. Insane!

When President Barack Hussein Obama was elected, everybody was proud and happy that for the first time; prejudices were put aside and people voted for a qualified candidate. He was not flawed, a Harvard graduate who spoke well, he was slim and healthy, he and his wife played basketball together, they went to the health club inside the WH. I assume they ate healthy food. They were raising their daughters to become educated, smart, and polite. They didn't have the appearance of being spoiled elites in any way. In other words, they were going to have to work to prosper and not just be given opportunities just because of their father's background...like some people we know.

During the time of President Obama's time in office. The wheels were turning for the Russian cyber infiltration. They set the time clock, and an explosion went off in America. Pundits were not ashamed to tell you how their stereotype schizophrenias about a black person came to light on national television shows. People like Glenn Beck, Judge Jeanine Ferris Pirro, Bill O'Reilly, Sean Hannity, Sarah Palin, Pastor Huckabee, Joe Scarborough, Pat Buchanan, Chris Christie, Rudy Giuliani, Lou Dobbs, Radio Host Hugh Hewitt, Kevin McCarthy, Tom Cotton, Paul Ryan, Steve King, Senator

Mitch McConnell, former Representative John Boehner and Eric Cantor. The list goes on and on and on. It's embarrassing. The money that some of FOX representatives are getting—was it from Russian oligarchs?

Chapter Eight

*****

The Russian Effect on 2016 Election

In the 1960's as I remember it in elementary school, we were taught that the Soviet Union and the Russians were coming to get us. We did drills at least once a month as I remember it. As a child climbing under my desk from the threat of a Russian attack, it was the farthest from our minds to become part of the Russian demographic. We could not have imagined that we would become "buddies."

No. 45 went to elementary school long before I did, and I know he had to go through the same drills the rest of us experienced. He was taught that Russia was the enemy and the United States government was not going to become friendly with their government any time in the future. Looking at any of the documentaries that

CNN has been showing about Russia lately, a picture is painted about why we should keep our distance. Now, why wouldn't No. 45 know that? And who are the millions of Americans that believe we should be friendly with that part of the country? It behooves me to think our country believes this is okay.

The documentaries being shown on television paints the picture of what it means to live in Russia and what Vladimir Putin represents. Are we getting besieged by digital media, as our country is going to hell in a handbasket, and Russia is the best country since peanut butter was discovered. It's one in the same to me.

These are the reasons that McCarthy went on a search for infiltrators in the U.S. government because he knew that there was something array and he had to spend the rest of his time in office making sure everyone knew it. However, he died of complications from alcoholism, allegedly.

It appears that No. 45 wants to find a scapegoat, he just keeps reaching backward to President Obama, who was the best President we ever had or ever will have. He just can't stand that people love him and respect him more than ever. The people who voted for President Obama knew what they were getting. Unlike this pot of dog crap we have today—which is too embarrassing to discuss or call his name. He somehow fooled the people into believing that he has the "keys" to get things done and make the world a better place.

It's all hogwash and gobbledygook. No. 45 is so unqualified for this job it is the height of hyperbole and bullshit—not a good mix.

Col. Lawrence Wilkerson, Retired U.S. Army is livid about the son of No. 45 sitting down with highly professional, highly decorated, highly knowledgeable and highly specialized military brass. These are long-time military professionals that know the demographics and players of the leaders that we must deal with in the world. We are surrounded by negative influences of conflict that wants to destroy America, and our government is pussy-footing around with amateurs from the Apollo show. It's crazy!

All this is by hiring family and close associates from the right-wing extremist regime is nothing more than No. 45 using the WH as his temple of gold like Saddam Hussein did during his reign. It's pathetic that he admires them so much, he rallies and gives embellishment to their dictatorships. No. 45 praised Hussein during the campaign. He said that he admired the dictator had his 'house in order.' In other words, No. 45 wanted to praise Saddam, but he stopped himself. Dumb!

Then there are the No. 45 campaign helpers who were so lame, no naïve and so desperate for money and success like Carter Page, who met with a Russian spy thinking it was a Russian businessman. Even if that is true—what were you thinking. I thought these people were sharp? This is what the New York Times wrote about Page on April 4, 2017.

Russian Spies Tried to Recruit Carter Page Before He Advised Trump

Russian intelligence operative tried in 2013 to recruit an American businessman and eventual foreign policy adviser to the Trump campaign who is now part of the F.B.I. The investigation into Russian's interference into the American election, according to federal court documents and a statement issued by the businessman.

The businessman, Carter Page, met with one of three Russian who was eventually charged with being undeclared officers with Russian's foreign intelligence service, known as the S.V.R. The F.B.I. Interviewed Mr. Page in 2013 as part of an investigation into the spy ring, but decided that he had not known the man was a spy, and the bureau never accused Mr. Page of wrongdoing.

The court documents say that Mr. Page, who founded an investment company in New York called Global Energy Capital, provided documents about the energy business to one of the Russian, Victor Podobnyy, think he was a businessman who could help with brokering deals in Russia.

In fact, Mr. Podobnyy was an S.V.R. officer posing as an attachés' the Russian mission to the United Nations. The court document does not identify Mr. Page, but the details in a statement he emailed to reporters on Tuesday match the individual described as "Male-1" in the court case. Mr. Pages' contact with the Russian spy was first reported on Monday by Buzz Feed News.

Read more…

https://www.nytimes.com/2017/04/04/us/politics/carter-page-trump-russia.html?ribbon-ad-idx=4&rref=politics&module=Ribbon&version=origin&region=Header&action=click&contentCollection=Politics&pgtype=article

Carter Page) was so naive that he was sitting down sharing information with the Russian's. Oh boy, and now we expect these people to know what they're doing in the WH? Joke! First off, most of us haven't traveled beyond Mexico or the Bahamas, how do we expect we could do business with a spy. We wouldn't know a spy if he said he was a "spy." Lol!

Paul Manafort has been accused of money laundering business over in Russia and is not surprising. If it's true, who is he laundering money for in the first place? Where are millions of dollars coming from. Let me not believe that the corporations for banks are laundering money from the high-octane drug sales going on in America—could that be? Is the banking industry closing a blind eye or becoming a part of the big net of drug dealers? Fishy!

If I didn't know any better, I would think that the banking industry is knowingly allowing these folks to put millions of dollars into accounts and are not tracking where it comes from. Why would a bank do that?

Read it for yourself below—

The headline of RedState.com said *Whoa. Say It Ain't So. Paul Manafort Embroiled In Money Laundering Scheme* March 21, 2017, by Streiff.

http://www.redstate.com/streiff/2017/03/21/whoa.-say-aint-so.-paul-manafort-embroiled-money-laundering-scheme/

Another runaway with an oligarch that thinks he is so smart and can also get away with anything. He almost did. In my opinion, it's a good thing No. 45 ran for office in 2016. He is being exposed, and his friends are too.

Then there is this--

Donald Trump's Many, Many, Many, Many Ties to Russia
Jeff Nesbit
Updated: Aug 15, 2016 10:39 AM ET | Originally published: Aug 02, 2016

Jeff Nesbit was the communications director to former Vice President Dan Quayle (R-IN) at the White House. He is the author of Poison Tea

http://time.com/4433880/donald-trump-ties-to-russia/

Read more…

Russian intelligence agencies have allegedly recently digitally **broken into** four different American organizations that are affiliated either with Hillary Clinton or the Democratic Party since late May. All of the hacks appear designed to benefit Donald Trump's presidential aspirations in one fashion or another.

When asked about this, and his affection for Russian President Vladimir Putin, Trump **said** any inference that a connection exists between the two is absurd and the stuff of conspiracy. "I have ZERO **investments in Russia**," he tweeted after the Democratic National Committee was apparently hacked by Russia and the emails released by Wiki Leaks on the eve of the DNC convention to nominate Clinton as its 2016 presidential candidate.

Most of the coverage of the links between Trump and Putin's Russia takes the GOP presidential nominee at his word—that he has lusted after a Trump Tower in Moscow, and come up spectacularly short. But Trump's dodge—that he has no businesses in Russia, so there is no connection to Putin—is a classic magician's trick. Show one idle hand, while the other is doing the work.

The truth, as several columnists and reporters have painstakingly **shown** since the first hack of a Clinton-affiliated group took place in late May or early June, is that several of Trump's businesses outside of Russia are entangled with Russian financiers inside Putin's circle.

So, yes, it's true that Trump has failed to land a business venture inside Russia. But the *real truth* is that, as major banks in America stopped lending him money following his many bankruptcies, the Trump organization was forced to seek financing from non-traditional institutions. Several had direct ties to Russian financial interests in ways that have raised eyebrows. What's more, several of Trump's senior advisors have business ties to Russia or its satellite politicians.

"The Trump-Russia links beneath the surface are even more extensive," Max Boot **wrote** in the Los Angeles TIMES. "Trump has sought and received funding from Russian investors for his business ventures, especially after most American banks stopped lending to him following his multiple bankruptcies."

*****

Summary of 2016 Election

■■

The election began going left in my view early on. Hillary Clinton seemed to come out later than previously when she ran against then Senator Obama. I still cannot figure out why that happened. Senator Bernie Sanders came out of nowhere and garnered millions of people that wanted to support him from nowhere. I am not sure if those were paid actors from the Trump campaign or just true Bernie Sanders supporters.

Next, No. 45 came out of the gate insulting Mexicans; they're rapist, they're not sending their best like you, and you, and you! I remember him saying we don't win anymore. Of course, he meant since President Obama was elected, he said we don't win. Yay, everybody takes a big bite off the cliché and rides off into the wind with No. 45, and a swath of Americans bit the apple.

What No. 45 is doing is handling the White House and the Constitution is not upholding what he swore on a bible that he would uphold. He is allowing his minions to run-a-muck in the WH, they are not trained, they are not lawyers, they are not seeking counsel, and so it goes—set yourself up for impeachment.

HRC came out and did her normal campaign speech; slowly, carefully, methodically. Just as she campaigned before. She's a nice lady. She's been inside and outside of politics for a very long time. Here is a newcomer with some quips and tricks up his sleeve and this country has the indifference to women in power and voters latched on like leeches.

The feminist movement did nothing in this election; they tried to fight the powers of the men that were telling women (especially men like Michael Flynn "trader" to his country) that she must go to jail, all along Flynn is lining his pockets with more money than you can imagine from Russia. Yet, he's chanting "lock her up." Trader!

Are the women voters going for this 'bait & switch' game in 2018? And what about 2020? We must confess— all that trash talk got you going. It stimulated you enough so you would get off your asses and go vote. Some of you have no idea how the process worked, and it took you aback; especially the electoral college process. I have been involved in politics for much of my life.

Obviously, people who had never voted before tricked themselves into believing this was normal behavior by No. 45. It was good that he was calling out Mexicans, the Muslims and making noise about what they were doing to America…and jobs. I personally don't hold anything against Mexicans. I just don't think like that when it comes to them holding me back from a job I want to pursue.

As a matter of fact, minorities are in competition with the entire country and most of them being Caucasian are in the Human Resources departments of these companies; who don't call you back, or waste time in an interview; knowing they have a friend of a friend or an internal candidate already waiting at his or her desk to be offered the job after you leave, or worse they never offer an opportunity to interview.

While I digress back to the election, it was an election from hell. It was a scene out of an Aliens movie; it was a production like no other production ever seen. It was historical racism, sexism, nationalism, extremism, bigotry, xenophobia, homophobia, and prejudices that seeped out of the mud of America like slim and creatures from the black lagoons.

While all the white men at No. 45s rallies spit on people, raised their fist to rally goers, pushed people, hollered out despicable names, kicked and screamed at strangers, threw objects, the women were holding their crouches (which I thought men only do among one another), they screamed and extorted their hot red faces under a tunnel of voters that had never been to a rally before or just didn't give a damn.

They were being side swiped and bamboozled into believing this was the way politics was supposed to be. I have been following and involved in politics for all of my adult life, and this is NOT normal behavior of a President. You saw the perfect example of it when President Obama was in office. Then we go from polished, intelligent, thoughtful, careful, legal-ease, no scandal to what we have now. If they didn't see it then—why would they see it now. After listening to the soft-spoken silence of President Obama—we just had to get what has been bottled up inside for eight years off of our chest I suppose. How ignorant did we must seem to the world? Whoa!

Let Us Not Forget the voices and faces of celebrities who rallied with someone they didn't know very well. Plus, they knew no third-party candidate has ever won the Presidency (ever), which is the choice of American voters. What threw me off was Professor Cornell West, movie producer Spike Lee, Rosie Rosario, Susan Sarandon, Michael Moore, Danny Glover, and Ben Jealous former NAACP President (not surprising) and others turned away from democratic values that supported African American and Hispanics for over 50 years.

They took a huge risk for a third-party candidate they didn't know well. You have all of them to thank for the demise of all the good that President Obama tried to do... especially for minorities and elderly, children, seniors, LGBTQ, and women. You don't see or hear from them much anymore. They had lots to do last summer. Hmm!

These are the policies and Executive Orders that are being overturned as we speak:

1. On his first day in office, President Donald Trump signed an executive order instructing federal agencies to minimize the burden of his predecessor's signature accomplishment, the Affordable Care Act, pending congressional repeal. *CBS News January 21, 2017*

2. And also, soon after he was sworn in, Mr. Trump signed an order to roll back a discount on the fees for a federal mortgage program that helps middle-class homebuyers. *CBS News January 21, 2017*

3. Issues like the Dakota Access Pipeline have been lightning rods of controversy, and are seen as indicative of an administration that regards the rights of Native Americans as dispensable. *By* **JESSICAH LAHITOU**, Bustle.com

4. Meals on Wheels has 3 percent of its budget provided by the federal government through the Community Development Block Grant Program. President Trump became aware of widespread, longstanding corruption and cronyism in that $3 Billion per year program and proposed that it be cut from the budget.

Go DanRiver.com Carolyn Winstead Bagley, March 28, 2017

Note* Here's why. Meals on Wheels programs get most of their federal funding through the Administration for Community Living, an agency of the Department of Health and Human Services that serves the elderly and disabled. That agency has a $227 million line-item for "home-delivered nutrition services."

Gregory Korte, USA TODAY Published 2:44 p.m. ET March 18, 2017, | Updated 5:34 p.m. ET March 19, 2017

Those programs are authorized through the Older Americans Act, a law so popular that its renewal passed Congress last year without any recorded opposition. And while Trump didn't single out that particular program, Health, and Human Services will receive a 16% across-the-board cut.

So, the celebrities that stood up against HRC and did damage to her numbers by supporting Senator Bernie Sanders (I) thank you, thank you, thank you! Americans whose seniors rely on those meals will never forget you. Let me say this to the millions of people that need Meals on Wheels for their elderly mother or father; while they're at work. Watch the damage control come out by summer of 2018 to give reasons why they are not at fault. Just thank them and keep moving on with your votes. When taking into consideration their voices. They're rich—living well!

Here's the Full List of Donald Trump's Executive Orders

By Avalon Zoppo NBC News April 2, 2017

http://www.nbcnews.com/politics/white-house/here-s-full-list-donald-trump-s-executive-orders-n720796

Church–

As long as our churches remain segregated on Sunday, there is no reason why the pastors should get involved in the politics of Washington unless their church is willing and prepared to invite everyone in on Sunday. Open the doors and let us all hear what is being preached on that day. They are collecting money and not paying taxes.

The parishioners or congregants are giving the preacher, Pastor, Rabbi, Priest, Cleric, Minister the money to live. They're able to buy cars, homes, boats, put their children through college on the dime of the church goers. I am not saying it's right or wrong. I'm saying that politics is not the place for them to expose their personal opinions. The words in the Bible should be their only salvation on Sunday. Not what this politician or that one expects you to do for *them*, especially when they are influencing hundreds of thousands of vulnerable believers each week.

Hollywood–

Like I said earlier in my book, celebrities are the 1% that you hear politicians speak about. They live well, and they are not wanting for anything. The elimination of *"Wheels on Meals"* does not affect them. But it does affect my 80-year-old neighbor and my 75-year-old Auntie or Uncle. A celebrity needs to stick to movies or singing or playing an instrument. It seems like they're doing us a favour, but really, they're not.

Past & Present Dangers–

I can write book-after-book and tell you how awful things are in America right now. The clear and present danger is the Russian ties that we have no business being involved in. I don't care what president of the United States is in office, to do business with an adversary is treason. We need to say that to our friends, family, and colleagues. The behavior you see from campaign associates like Carter Page and Paul Manafort's business dealings border on trading information and talking to spies they claim they don't even know are spies, which is even worse.

We need to watch what is going on and stop lying to ourselves, trying to trick our minds into saying, "What we are seeing is not a Russian infiltration." It is! We don't value America apparently, because had this been in the 1940s, 1950s, 1960s, and beyond, we would be preparing to go to war with the Soviet Union. I cannot believe that America is letting this all go down and not yelling to the highest of all voices by protesting or doing more than tweeting?

Congresswoman Maxine Waters (CA) has it right. There are too many inconsistencies, conflicts, discrepancies, and incongruities around this election of No. 45. He is using the WH as a place to conjure up business for the Trump Foundation/Organization. He is going to Mara-Largo Florida to meet-and-greet with heads of countries (who normally visit at the WH) to avoid pictures and signing in to show who he met.

Is any American asking why? Every time he goes to Florida the taxpayer is being asked to pay for secret service. What are you going to do about it? Why is his wife living in another location? Is she running a separate business operation? Nobody asked.

Hence, all the negatives that No. 45 brought to your attention during his campaign and every word he spoke negatively about HRC was all about his insufficiencies and illegalities. Where are those tax returns? Why are we not pushing our Congressmen to subpoena his tax returns?

I don't have a lot of hope for what's going to come out of the F.B.I. counterintelligence investigation. I do believe people will take the hit for the current President and they will say what Carter Page said and they will get away with making business deals with Russia. I believe they are making it look like this is what we should be doing—normalizing doing business with a communist country and dictator like Vladimir Putin.

It's a slap in the face to our soldiers who have worked and died to keep us safe from oligarchs and murderous enemies like the ones we are facing now. The country is in danger of collapsing from within by people who claim; they will make America great again.

Who said it wasn't great already? Because a black man became President of the United States?

We should be shaking our heads in shame and not rallying behind this man who chose to do business with a sworn enemy. Whether you want to accept it or not, this is where we are, my friends.

*****

SMH

I have nothing further to add!!

The Write Format II

info@thewriteformat2books.com

www.thewriteformat2.com

Tracy T. B.